Keys

to the room:

UNLOCKING THE DOORS TO OPPORTUNITIES AND POSSIBILITIES

THOUGHTS AND
INSIGHTS ON
ENTREPRENEURSHIP
AND HOSPITALITY

JOHN OPPENHEIMER

Library of Congress Control Number: 2011963211
CreateSpace Independent Publishing Platform,
North Charleston, South Carolina

ISBN: 1468112546
ISBN-13: 9781468112542

Printed in the United States of America.

10 9 8 7 6 5 4 3 2 1

Second Edition

Requests for permission to use all or any portion of this work should be mailed to:

Columbia Hospitality
2200 Alaskan Way, Suite 200
Seattle WA 98121

KEYS TO THE ROOM
Unlocking the Doors to Opportunities and Possibilities

Thoughts and Insights on Entrepreneurship and Hospitality

Doors carry a lot of symbolism in business. I like it when hard work pays off and a closed door opens; that means there's an opportunity ahead. The key is to recognize the opportunity, be it small or large, a loud declaration or a barely audible whisper. When doors close, that tends to indicate an ending, which is always followed by a new beginning. Some doors slam shut—perhaps a lesson in disguise. If you don't pick up on that, you may find yourself caught in a revolving door. And there's no key to get out of that.

DEDICATION

This collection of stories is dedicated to both my personal and professional families.

Specifically, I honor my wife, Deanna, daughter, Jeni, son, James, and my late parents, Jane and Arthur Oppenheimer—all of whom provided special inspiration and long-lasting lessons that I continue to learn and practice today.

TABLE OF CONTENTS

FOREWORD

It's been my privilege for the last thirty-five years to be involved in five entrepreneurial companies, each of which I'm proud to say is still in business today. Each provided opportunities for team members and livelihoods for families and extraordinary service to clients and guests. The organizations have centered around events and hospitality. The companies, in the order of their inception, include:

- CRG Events—specializes in organizing corporate events throughout the world.
- Columbia Hospitality (the company I'm most involved in)—specializes in managing distinctive venues, hotels and resorts, public

and private golf courses, residential properties, and conference centers.

- Cruise Terminals of America—operates within a unique partnership with General Steamship Agencies and SSA Marine and exclusively operates two cruise terminals in Seattle, Washington.
- Seattle Hotel Group—developed and owns the Four Seasons Seattle Hotel.
- Oppenheimer Ventures—invests in hospitality properties and services.

Together, these companies have employed more than three thousand people, many of whom have developed and grown into the new leadership and have taken the companies further than I ever dreamed.

Back in 2005, Deanna, my wife of thirty-two years, worked as one of the top executives at financial giant Barclays, based in London. She and I divided our time between Seattle and London to take advantage of the unique career opportunities afforded us in both parts of the world. That situation is what led me to write down some thoughts on opening and closing doors in the hospitality industry. Put more simply, I had a lot of time on planes and lots of time to think, so why not put it down on paper?

Therefore, with the help of my friend Teri Citterman, who is a Seattle-based freelance writer, and Amy McBride, who is an amazing colleague at Columbia Hospitality, here are some anecdotes about what has helped our small businesses succeed.

The Keys to the Room

Every time I slide my key into the slot of my hotel room door and the little green light comes on, I feel anxious, and I mean that in a good way. When I walk through the door, I'm hoping to enter perfection. I'm looking forward to the peace and quiet, a restful night's sleep in a bed that's perfectly made—soft and warm and luxurious. Be it business or pleasure, I'm looking for a respite. I'm looking for an experience different from my everyday life.

At Columbia Hospitality, our business delivers that experience, that perfection—ensuring everyone has an amazing time. Every time a guest walks through the doors of one of the properties we manage, our job is to make his or her time with us fun, entertaining, and memorable. Every day, our team members have the ability to make lifelong memories for guests. We get to be a part of some of their most important occasions in life, like weddings, birthdays, and anniversaries. We also have the privilege of hosting product launches, employee meetings, and stockholder meetings for some of the largest companies in the world.

Tall order? Sometimes.

As the chief executive officer of a hospitality company, I spend a lot of time thinking about a guest's experience and how to fill that tall order. How can we deliver perfection? Our proven method is by following our values:

Honesty, Sincerity, Respect, Creativity, Enthusiasm, and Accountability.

They are the answers and the approach we take toward delivering that perfect experience every time a guest walks through our doors. This book is a collection of stories, insights, and experiences of the wisdom I've accumulated as a CEO, an entrepreneur, a colleague, a husband, father, son, brother, and friend. They are the keys that I've used to unlock numerous doors to great opportunities.

WHEN A DOOR OPENS—
WALK THROUGH IT!

Forming Columbia Hospitality was based on the premise that we needed to dream big and figure it out as we went. And that outlook permeates our culture to this day. One of the things I most admire about our executive team is that each one as an individual really knows opportunity when he or she sees it. We don't second-guess. We go for it!

- When we started, we'd never operated an event facility, but we dreamed of managing venues. Now we manage distinctive venues, conference centers, hotels, resorts, spas, restaurants, residential properties, and golf courses.

- One team member, Leasa Mayer, a twenty-two-year business partner, dreamed of being a CEO. When we spun off the original event company, she became, and currently still is, the CEO and majority owner of CRG Events.
- Bret Matteson, Columbia Hospitality's former president, thought it would be challenging to do an international project—and opened the door to oversee the development and management of multiple properties in Portugal.
- One evening over cocktails, Sasha Nosecchi, our Director of Retail Innovation, learned her friend's company hoped to take a 100+ year old building in Seattle, The Smith Tower, and turn it into an iconic event center. Instead of simply listening and never giving it a second thought, Sasha took the next step and introduced many of us to her friend's company, which led to us managing a new exciting venue in Seattle!
- Since 2006 we'd been meeting with Shawn Cucciardi, a golf professional and partner in several golf courses in the Northwest, to explore a partnership. Shawn had teamed up with Ryan Moore, a professional PGA golfer and his family to form RMG. It took 10 years, but we knew in our heart of hearts that Columbia, Shawn and RMG could do

great things together. Today, Shawn is our Director of Golf Operations, we manage and have invested in RMG's courses, and have partnered with Mike Moore (Ryan's dad) to source new courses.

And there's one more side to this story. If team members' dreams are not achievable at our organization, then we try and help them find places where they can fulfill them. Two things can happen: either they become amazingly successful and happy because they're doing what they love, or they realize their dream wasn't what they wanted after all, and they come back. I can't stress enough the importance of keeping in touch with great team members, even when they leave—*especially* when they leave. The future is wide open, and if you give them a great reason to miss you, you never know what can happen. I always tell great team members whom we're sad to see go that "the door is always open to come back home," and it's amazing how many do. That's not to say I'm not extremely sad when good people leave. I take it far too personally and see it as a failure on our part. On the other hand, I love it when good colleagues come back.

FOCUS ON
WHAT YOU KNOW

In 1988, I got a call from Bruce Chapman, who, at the time, worked for the Hudson Institute. Bruce was a former State of Washington secretary of state, a former prominent Seattle city councilman, and director of the U.S. Census. In other words, Bruce was an important guy. He invited me to a dinner at a fancy restaurant in Seattle with Paul Schell, who was running for Port of Seattle commissioner, and venture capitalist Tom Alberg. I didn't know any of them and thought he had me confused with someone else who he really meant to invite. But I decided to go, because at the time, I'd never be able to eat at that restaurant unless someone else picked up the check!

I had moved an event-planning company called Columbia Resource Group (CRG Events) to Seattle from Washington, D.C., and Paul wanted to pick my brain as an event planner. In his run for port commissioner, he had a vision of revitalizing the Seattle waterfront by tearing down some dilapidated buildings and replacing them with a hotel and a conference center. He wanted to make it a walkable waterfront and livable destination.

When I got home from the dinner, I told Deanna, "I just met the most interesting man. He's running for some office I've never heard of, and he has really big ideas. Too bad he's never going to get elected." Little did I know he would get elected, the waterfront would be transformed as he envisioned, and he would help me launch Columbia Hospitality.

The Port of Seattle retained CRG Events as a consultant to assist in defining what makes a world-class conference center. At the time we had worked all over the world planning events, so we had a few opinions regarding venues. When the decision was made to build the conference center, the Port put the project out for bid for an operator. We didn't have experience managing conference centers, so we didn't submit a proposal. The Port ended up hiring a company from Texas to run the conference center, but it didn't work out. They put the bid out again, and we decided to change our perspective. Rather than focusing on what we thought we didn't know, we focused on what we did know. We knew the customer and we knew what would make a great, profitable center.

Given that we were event planners, we brought a deep understanding of what event planners wanted from an event space. We were local and we were entrepreneurial, and we believed we could create a local hallmark out of the conference center for the waterfront. But the Port would have to take a risk, which is counter to most bureaucracies. Surprising us all, they took it and hired us.

As a result, we founded Columbia Hospitality and launched a hospitality management company. Today, we still run Bell Harbor International Conference Center. It was profitable from the start—so it never required the Port to subsidize it. Paul went on to be elected mayor of Seattle. He owned three boutique hotels, and he turned over the management of them to us.

Was it luck, timing, or the seizing of an opportunity when the door opened? Probably a little of each. Paul, Tom, and I became good friends and have enjoyed being business partners together on various projects throughout the years. What's funny to me is none of them remember that dinner.

MAKE SUCCESS FROM A MESS

Makes me think of Sting's song—with *my* lyrics: "Every move you make, every *job you take*, every *mess* you make…*they'll* be watching you."

When we built Cedarbrook Conference Center near SeaTac airport outside of Seattle, we were under the proverbial microscope and deservedly so. We disrupted the neighborhood for more than a little while with our cranes and bulldozers. Nearby neighbors had little choice but to endure the dust and gravel, jackhammering, and drilling. It was dirty and loud, and there was nothing they could do about it.

But there was something *we* could do. We created the mess and, in doing so, we created an opportunity. One morning while it was still dark, people in hardhats scurried from house to house leaving bags of bagels and cream cheese at each front door with a note attached: *Thanks for putting up with us.*

This was a simple gesture—cheap and easy—and we had fun doing it. We wanted them to know how much we appreciated their patience. We wanted them to know we didn't take them for granted. And the amount of goodwill it garnered in the neighborhood was immeasurable. The glares and honks turned to smiles and waves. Success!

Time passed and all was well. We continued to break and hammer concrete and be an utter nuisance. The goodwill with the neighbors gently faded, and it was time for a new note of thanks. On Valentine's Day, every household received a big basket of heart-shaped cookies on their doorstep with a giant *thank-you* note. Again, this was a simple, cheap, and easy gesture, but it was incredibly meaningful to the community.

When we finally finished the project, one of the neighbors came through to take a tour. "Now that the center is built, does this mean we're not going to wake up to any more goodies?" You know you've had an impact when you get a response like that. A mess is a mess only if you overlook it as an opportunity.

DO IT!

Can you ever *plan* for a change in plans? I think if you're open-minded and flexible, the payoff can be huge. In late 2010, my mom passed away and as I spoke at her memorial, I recalled "Mom's Magnificent Lessons." Number five was "You never know what's going to happen when you wake up," and it's one of my personal mantras. Throughout my life, my mom had a fantastic way of answering, "Sure, sounds great, let's do it," to whatever impromptu idea I had.

Life is frenetic in nature and can be ambiguous at times. I believe in grabbing and tackling opportunities when they come. But for some people, ambiguity is a big challenge. I try to encourage team members—and myself—to be ready for the opportunities that challenge inevitably brings.

Professionally, I'm not a huge believer in five-year plans, because some of the best businesses I've been a part of—and had the most fun at—would never have gotten off the ground with a time-specific strategic plan.

The same holds true for opportunities with family. When Deanna received the offer to head Barclays in London, we had a decision to make (I'll talk more about that later.) It would be a challenge and an opportunity. It sounded great. We decided to do it and divide our time between two great cities.

Certainly, having one spouse working in London and another based in Seattle most of the time forced us to adapt. Our entire family came to value our time together even more than we used to. We also knew that Seattle was our home and our London-Seattle lifestyle was not something that would last forever. So we enjoyed it and took advantage of every moment. We seized the chance and adapted to change. What an extraordinary opportunity it was for all of us; not always easy, but I would do it again in a heartbeat.

REINVENT EVERY DAY

I've been in the business of hospitality for a long time, and I think it's fair to say I'm a one-career guy. There is no end for an entrepreneur, only opportunities to expand and innovate.

It's important to never get comfortable in your job. The saying goes, "Live every day like it's your last," but in a career, I think it's best to approach every day like it's your first.

When an enthusiastic team member walks through the door, the energy is contagious. And when we're in that mind-set, we're able to see all those little opportunities to make great things happen. It's compelling and creates a great work atmosphere, and guests love to see it.

Every time we renew our management contracts, we go to great lengths to convince the property owners, some of whom we've had contracts with for years, that today we're as fresh and enthusiastic as we were the first time we signed the contract. They need to know that we are energized—with the fire in our bellies that we had when they were brand new clients. We are most successful when we look at each opportunity as if it is our first and only shot.

The ease of entry into hospitality is simple—but to guard against the competition, we have to perform as if we're new to the stage. Opening night is every night, and we must bring new ideas and new approaches to the table every time we are invited to sit down.

LEARN SOMETHING OLD

Reinvention is a big theme around Columbia Hospitality. We do it for our guests, and we should do it for ourselves. Unfortunately, it's easy to get bogged down and drop that idea all the way to the bottom of the priority list. A few years ago I decided I was getting a little too far away from our day-to-day operations. I wanted a better understanding of what's going on at our various properties and within our various departments, so I blocked my schedule and decided to do some "job shadowing"—following team members around for the day to see firsthand how they do their jobs, what challenges they face, and what improvement could be made.

One day, I showed up at one of our hotels and met with the general manager. I told him I was ready to do whatever was on his calendar that day. I was going to hang out with him and be his shadow. I'm not sure how thrilled he was about this idea, but sometimes surprises are a great way to connect with people. I attended department meetings, candidate interviews, and dining room team member lineups. I participated in the property's marketing conference call, hung out with the chefs in the kitchen, and then spent part of the day with the director of housekeeping, walking the property and auditing the guest rooms. The whole day was a great experience.

Next, I went to an all-day new employee orientation. I used to go to these all the time, but they fell off my radar. It was a great opportunity for me to get reenergized—to get back in touch with that raw enthusiasm and excitement of what it's like to be a new team member at Columbia Hospitality.

More recently, I spent an afternoon at Salish Lodge making pizzas in the open wood-burning oven with our Executive Chef, Matt Heikkila, and Lead Cook, Matt Anderson. Not only did I learn to make great pizzas, but I was reminded how hard our chefs multitask. It's not easy juggling dozens of items at the same time.

The couple of days I spent with team members reminded me that we *can* always learn something old again. While my role may be important to the company, really, by far, the most important people are the general managers, the housekeepers, the line chefs, and all the others who shape the time guests spend with us. These team members are the most powerful people in our company. They make the smallest differences in every guest's experience, and that's a *very* big deal.

MAKE YOUR BED

I'm a big believer in the little things. Paying attention to them always makes a guest's experience a positive one, but not paying attention to them, even just once, can crush a hotel's reputation.

When I first began my career, I received an unusual lesson in the details of organization from an early roommate. Scott Jackson has been a friend for nearly four decades and is still one of my closest. At the time, when Scott and I lived in Washington, D.C., every morning I'd rush around with my toothbrush in one hand and my coffee cup in the other—trying to balance spitting the toothpaste and swallowing the coffee.

On certain days, when things were particularly hectic, I'd get a call around midmorning from Scott. "How's your day going?" he'd ask. Inevitably, right at the time he'd call, I'd be in a spiral of pandemonium. It got weirdly predictable. Finally, I asked, "How is it that you always know when I'm in the middle of absolute chaos?"

"You didn't make your bed," he'd tell me. Scott's philosophy was you couldn't leave the house without making your bed. It's unorganized and screws up your whole day. He was right. (OK, one day he refolded all the clothes in my dresser, but that's a whole other set of issues).

Now, a made bed symbolizes organization to me—and an organized mind leads to an organized desk, which leads to a lot more productivity. That was a pretty valuable lesson Scott taught me. Today and every day, I don't leave the house without making the bed. For me, it's key to start the day with an organized bed, which leads to an organized day. I recognize that for others, starting the day with a double espresso can lead to the same thing.

CHANNEL FRANCK

One of my favorite movies is *Father of the Bride,* but it's not so much the movie I love. It's the character of Franck Eggelhoffer. Pronounced "Fr-aaaah-nck Eggelhoffer," he's the wedding planner, played by Martin Short, who was wacky and fanatical about details. That's me.

I like it when the water bottles in the fridge are lined up with their labels facing forward. Some people say I'm right there with the other two million Americans with obsessive-compulsive tendencies. I agree. But it doesn't take that much of an extra effort to turn the bottles facing out. It's organized and it shows you paid attention. It's a little detail that can mean a lot to every person who opens the fridge.

Franck knew his strengths. He didn't try to be the dressmaker or make wedding cakes. He knew his role and expected nothing less than perfection from himself and those around him. When he took on a bride as a client, he became part of the family. He was there to anticipate, celebrate, and clean up big messes. As in business and in life, I think the most successful partnerships are those that have clearly outlined separate roles and responsibilities. Most of the time, though not all the time, I think it's key to stick to those duties that are assigned to you.

When our children were young, Deanna was in charge of packing their lunches. One day, she was out of town, so the lunch packing fell to me. I thought it'd be a fun surprise for Jeni, our second grader, to pack a bottle of root beer in her lunch. In a rush, I threw in a bottle, neglecting to notice the word "root" was absent from the label. Later, around noon, Jeni called and asked, "Dad, why did you put a bottle of beer in my lunch?"

I did not channel Franck very well that day.

CALL BACK IN TEN

If I can't answer a call within three rings, I try to call people back within ten minutes of receiving their voice mail. People don't expect that. E-mail has replaced ear-to-ear conversation and, unfortunately, a lot can get lost in its translation.

Granted, it's not always possible to call back that quickly, but I do know that if you call someone back within ten minutes of him or her leaving you a voice mail, the response you get is very different than when you wait an hour or a whole day. Since I've been doing this, I've received an amazing response. It's such a simple gesture, and yet people are genuinely surprised, sometimes shocked. What I want them to feel is important. I want them to know that I have a sense of urgency on their behalf. When they feel this way, you can have a huge impact.

The other day, our receptionist took a call from a guest who had a complaint about her stay at one of our island properties. The guest called our main number looking for our vice president of operations, who was out of the office. The receptionist relayed the conversation to me, and I picked up the phone and called the guest back. Boy, was she surprised to get a call from the CEO less than five minutes after initially leaving her message. It's not always easy to pick up the phone when you know you're calling someone who is upset, but can you imagine how much more upset she would have become if she'd had to wait longer to be heard? She would have had more time to share her negative experience with others and her frustration would have grown. The simple act of immediately calling back demonstrated to her that we took her concerns very seriously, and this alone can make all the difference.

As another example, I received a call from a woman who wanted to arrange for her daughter and herself to stay at Salish Lodge. I called our general manager, and he called her back within minutes to make the arrangements and find out what we could do to make her stay special. We made her feel important. She went on to have a wonderful time during her stay and spent lots of money in the spa, the dining room, and the gift shop. She had felt so special from the beginning that it carried through her stay. This epitomizes the sense of urgency I want each of our team members to demonstrate on behalf of our guests. I want each guest to feel as if he or she is royalty—at least while he or she is a guest with us.

BROADCAST YOUR VALUES

Reputation is the biggest asset a person or a company has. Yet history shows that companies often write down their values, then stash them away, hoping a crisis never occurs to make them accountable to them. I look at it differently. Values are the key to our reputation. And sometimes an opportunity doesn't fit our values—which means it's best to let that door close.

I want everyone to know our values—every guest, every team member, every potential team member, every vendor, every investor, every partner, every family member…the world! I want everyone to know, so it makes it that much easier for us to hold ourselves to them. Our values influence how we make decisions and act as a company. Just like the personal values you develop as an individual, our values are the litmus test for everything we do. They guide our attitude, our actions, and how we conduct ourselves every second. If our values are known, both internally and externally, there is very little room for bad judgment.

Again, those Columbia Hospitality Values are and always have been:

Honesty, Sincerity, Respect, Creativity, Enthusiasm, and Accountability.

In addition to our values, our mission and mantra is O.M.G.(!)

Own the values.

Make it fun.

Get it done.

EXPECT LOYALTY

When people join our organization, they become part of the Columbia Hospitality family. And just like checking in with a sibling, I love checking in to see how the company is meeting team members' goals and needs.

Some people wonder if it's realistic to expect complete loyalty from every team member. I think it absolutely is, but I can't expect a team member to be loyal to us if we're not loyal to him or her. That is why it's so important to us that we invest in team members' development, recognize and reward their achievements, and empower them to make values-based decisions on their own. When team members know we are loyal to them, then I'm confident that the decisions they make are good for the guests, the rest of the team, and the company, not just for them as individuals.

It's human instinct to think that the world revolves around us as individuals. It's hard to think about situations in terms of *us*—not you or me. But those who succeed in business think exactly that way. When we, as a company, act in the best interests of our property owners, guests, and team members at the exclusion of none of them, it's the greatest expression of our loyalty to them.

APPLAUD MISTAKES

Some people view hospitality as an industry that is slow to adapt and change.

In fact, I think it's one of the most dynamic industries. Almost every day, a new challenge arises, and along with it the opportunity to learn. I've been known to say that as long as we're decisive, it's OK to make mistakes. In fact, it's mistakes that often drive our success. Here's how we do it. On Monday, we make a decision and proceed. On Wednesday, we evaluate whether that decision was the right one and if we're seeing the results we want. If not, by Friday, we read-just or change it. I'd say that's pretty dynamic.

This creates an environment where people jump in, pay attention, and take risks. I see too many companies that don't encourage or empower employees to take risks because they might make a mistake. I don't want to be one of those companies. For us, as long as we keep learning, mistakes are not punished; they're applauded.

FAIL TO SUCCEED

No one likes to fail, and it's hard not to personalize it. As an example, one of our residential properties experienced some turmoil when a valued team member resigned. Not having all the information, the homeowners questioned the circumstances surrounding the team member's departure and the frustration quickly spun out of control. In the course of a weekend it seemed like our over ten years of success at this property might be in jeopardy. We took the criticism very personally but knew we needed to act fast. We scheduled a meeting with the homeowners for early Monday morning and a couple members of our leadership team and I addressed the concerns head-on. Clearly we had failed along the way for the situation to reach this level of frustration, but it gave us an opportunity to succeed and we learned a lot from the open dialogue that day.

Now, I'm not going to suggest we solved everything in that meeting but it was the start to a better understanding of how we can improve the home-owner experience. Today, we're still learning how to continue to build on that information. Sometimes we have to fail in order to succeed.

VALUE TIME

Punctuality is a pet peeve of mine. I like people who are on time, and I try at all costs to be on time as well. But sometimes life happens, and sometimes you can't help it. You're going to be late.

Once a potential client contacted us asking if we could run his hotel in Portland. It was a big opportunity, so we drove 172 miles to his office. After three hours in the car, we arrived at his office on the Willamette River and waited. We waited for two hours, until he finally called to tell us he wouldn't make it to the meeting. It was shocking. We knew this was probably someone we would not want to do business with in the future.

When you're late, you send a clear message to the person who's waiting: My time is worth more than yours. They can just sit and wait—and you'll get there when you get there, *if* you get there. Wow. There are a lot of people in this world who think this way, but that is not how we think at Columbia Hospitality. Eventually, the client from Portland contacted us again about a piece of property he wanted to sell. We politely declined his inquiry. We felt our time would be better served on a client who valued it.

Sometimes, people can't control being late, but you can control how you make them feel about it. The other day, I was scheduled to meet with an executive from another company. He called to let me know he had a flat tire and was going to be late. At that moment, I knew my only job was to make him feel like a million bucks!

HAVE THE
COURAGE TO LISTEN

They don't call it "thorn in your side" for nothing. Intuition, your gut, is a powerful tool that many people fail to use enough. And when you don't use it, things can get tricky.

The nonessential clutter in our lives keeps us from listening to our gut. In today's world of mobile devices, e-mail and text messaging, we're presented with an overwhelming amount of information and are expected to read, digest, and comment back immediately. Everything seems urgent! Taking time to form original thoughts, let alone tap into your inner gut, is nearly impossible on this timeline. Or maybe it isn't. Your gut is immediate. It's how you respond—your "gut reaction." It's in this very environment where intuition is most needed as a guide to help us know when to say yes—and when not to.

In business, hiring decisions are an area where following your intuition can really pay off! That's true for both parties. In the past, there were a handful of cases when our senior team had reservations about hiring a candidate. We couldn't quite put our finger on why, so we hired the person. Without exception, it was the wrong thing to do for the company and for that team member. We learned that even if a candidate looks great on paper and interviews well, we have to trust our instincts and know when to close the door. If our gut says, "Don't do it," we have to have the courage to listen.

FORGET AND
THEY'LL REMEMBER

I think one of the most embarrassing things some-one can do is meet you for, let's say, the third time, and *still* not remember your name. I actually feel embarrassed for that person. We've all got stuff on our minds, but I'm pretty sure that after the third time meeting someone—myself included—you might want to make a bigger effort.

When I meet someone, I try to focus on his or her eyes. I find it's very difficult for me to forget some-one when he or she maintains eye contact. I also think it's a great opportunity for you to listen with both ears and be seriously focused on that person. If the circumstances are right, ask the right question to get him or her to tell a personal story. That's a great way to remember people and a window through which to see a completely different side of a person.

Most people take it for granted that you'll remember their names. And, frankly, it's the least you can do. But forgetting a name—well, you just look like a jerk—especially after the third time meeting them. You can count on the fact that that door, which was beginning to open, has now perpetually slammed shut.

GIVE UP YOUR SOCKS

We can and will do anything! We don't even mind breaking rules as long as we stay true to our values.

One evening, a guest showed up with a horrified look on her face. It was about 11:30 p.m., and she was checking into one of our properties. Gary, one of our team members, inquired of the guest if anything was wrong. The guest had flown in for a job interview—her dream job, no less—and realized she'd forgotten to bring socks. The interview was scheduled for first thing the next morning. Our guest was in a pickle! And Gary had some choices:

- Wish her luck and send her on her way, adding, "Don't let the door hit'cha on the backside."
- Give her the socks he was wearing, noting desperate times call for desperate measures.
- Or, figure out what, if anything, he could do to get new dress socks to the woman by the next morning.

Gary acted quickly and reassured the guest she could expect a new pair of socks delivered to her room in time for her interview. Gary jumped into his car and headed off to the nearest twenty-four-hour store for the socks, but not before sending a glass of complimentary wine to the guest's room with a note saying, "Relax, we'll make sure you're prepared to knock *their* socks off tomorrow!" We don't know if the guest got the job, but we do know she was not interviewing barefoot as she had feared.

GET WET

It was a beautiful summer day at Cedarbrook Conference Center, and Boeing employees attending a company event were about to enjoy a relaxing outdoor reception on the Grand Lawn. Our banquet team members had just finished their preparations and were "at attention," waiting to receive our guests.

Just as they started to arrive, the automatic sprinkler system turned on around the perimeter of the event. Without hesitation and within a split second, one of our service team members jumped between the guests and the oncoming water, serving as a human shield.

The guests observed this with gratitude and amaze-ment while Miguel stood there smiling and get-ting soaked until the sprinkler system was shut down.

FIND THE FRESCA

A team member was taking an order at one of our restaurants, and a guest said he'd like to have a Fresca—you know the soft drink you never see anymore? Our restaurant didn't have one on hand or anywhere in storage, but our server told the guest he'd see what he could do. Five minutes later, he returned from a trip to a convenience store with a hard-to-find Fresca in hand. The guest was ecstatic!

THROW PARTIES!
HOST SLEEPOVERS!

What is hospitality?

- Yes, it's the cordial and generous reception of guests.
- Yes, it's a wide range of activities, each dedicated to the service of people away from home.
- Yes, it's making people feel welcome in your space, providing them food and drink, and making sure they are comfortable.
- And yes, I'm asleep, because while those are correct, they are all very boring definitions.

I chose hospitality because I love it. In high school and college, I was very social and an organizer, so it's no real surprise that I chose the business of throwing parties and events. When people attend, they already want to have a good time and be productive—our job is simply to enhance their experience as much as we can. I'm the classic example of someone doing something he loves.

Being in the business of fun, we get to entertain! Throw parties! Host sleepovers! Every day and every night of the year, our job is to make sure every single person we come in contact with has the time of his or her life from the moment he or she arrives until the person's tearful departure (*Yes!* That's how moved we want them to be—over and over and over.) Our job is to make him or her feel exceedingly special.

We want every guest to feel he or she is the most important person we've ever had stay with us. In fact, we want him or her to feel like he or she is the *only* guest we have right now. That's how special! Out of all the options our guests have for a venue to hold their meetings, have their weddings, or spend their free time, when they choose us we feel honored. But with that honor comes a huge responsibility to make it special, make it memorable, and confirm they made the right choice.

CREATE BILLBOARDS

We are in the *guest* business. And we want our guests to be in the billboard business. We want every person who comes into contact with us to tell his or her friends stories about his or her experience. So it is our job to create compelling stories for every guest...and for each other. That is, we try to create such positive experiences for our guests and team members that they become evangelical about sharing their stories with family, friends, and business associates. We want raving fans inside and outside our company. Those stories are our language—they're our billboards.

Every day, I task myself and each team member to create two signature stories: one for a guest and one for a colleague. These stories are the fabric of our company, and we have the unique opportunity to reinvent ourselves every day. How many companies are lucky enough to say that? Here's a great story:

Three generations of women from the same family entered the Spa at Salish Lodge. The mother and daughter had an appointment for a heated river rock massage treatment. Accompanying them in a wheelchair was the elderly family matriarch, unable to fully lift her head or speak. Her daughter asked to have her elderly mother in the room while the service took place, and Aaron, the massage practitioner, was informed of the situation. During the treatment, instead of simply leaving the grandmother alone to watch, Aaron took a few of the warm stones and moved them down her arms. Then, he placed them in her hands. Unable to speak to Aaron, the woman expressed sounds of joy. Following the treatment, Aaron approached the grandmother, opened up her hand, and placed a heart-shaped stone in her palm. He told her he handpicks each of the stones he uses, and he wanted her to have this special one, explaining how to warm it and use it to relieve aches and pains. The woman smiled, and her eyes filled with tears. Her daughter was blown away by Aaron's gesture. She explained that her mother had collected heart-shaped stones since she was a child, and was now almost ninety years old. Needless to say, there wasn't a dry eye in the place. Aaron made magical memories that day!

HIRE GREATNESS

Finding the right team members is a challenge for every company. I've seen great companies (including ours) hire the total wrong-fit candidates and great candidates get passed over for perfect-fit positions. Interviewing is an art and a science. We want to work with people who are dynamic and fun, and who embrace our values, and who radiate positive energy.

When I'm considering hiring a candidate, I ask myself, if I were on a plane to London (nine-ish hours), and the candidate were seated next to me, would I be happy, sad, or terrified if he or she struck up a conversation with me? At the end of every interview, I evaluate the quality of our conversation by finishing the following sentence:

If I were sitting next to this candidate on a plane, I would…

- Pull out my book and stare at it intensely.
- Pretend to be asleep.
- Pretend I don't speak English.
- Engage.

If I could envision our conversation as seatmates, chances are the candidate would make a great team member. In business, as in our personal lives, life is too short to spend time with people who don't give us joy and are nothing short of a complete pleasure to be around. I'm not saying we sit around every day singing "Kumbaya," but I like knowing we could if we wanted to.

BE GRACIOUS

Well, we are in the business of making people feel special, and that trickles through every property we manage, as well as our own internal organization. From the time a candidate walks through our doors for an interview, we want him or her to feel like he or she is the most important guest to ever enter the building. We enthusiastically welcome candidates, call them by their name (and remember it), take care of their needs, and thank them at the end for coming in. They may not get the job, but at some point, they *might* be a guest at one of our restaurants or at one of our properties. When people are treated graciously, they remember it; they remember it even more when they are not.

A few years back, I was in a meeting with a roomful of lawyers. One woman stood out as someone who seemed fair and good to work with. After five weeks of meeting together, she told me we had met twelve years ago. She was exploring opportunities and we'd apparently done an informational interview. She said what stood out in her memory was how gracious I had been. I felt great knowing she felt good about meeting with me, yet terrible for not remembering it. You just never know who will be your next team member, your next guest, or the next attorney sitting across the room from you. It's important to always make a great impression, because you just never know.

FIND DIAMONDS

I want to do a better job discovering the gems in our organization. As we grow, we need to work harder to spot them. It seems that growth would make it easier, because there are more people. But that's not the case. Every day is a test to stay connected to each team member—our servers, our housekeepers, our set-up crew—and spot potential. We've found servers whom we've developed into great leaders. When we were smaller, it was easier. As we grow, it's more difficult, but I know there are team members throughout our organization who will make amazing company leaders.

It's not my style to micromanage or hold the reins on hiring, except when it comes to hiring our concierges. Until recently, almost every concierge interviewed with me, and I rejected 40 percent of the final candidates. It's one of the most important hires we make. I'll forgo the opportunity to weigh in on the director of communications or a sales associate, but with a concierge candidate, I know what I want and my expectations are very specific.

I've heard research cited that says seven to seventeen seconds is all you have to make a first impression. A concierge's first impression is critical. In an interview, I want to see enthusiasm. I want to know who specifically, met with them from our team. I know he or she has had a long day of interviews and is probably exhausted. But I want to see high energy—because all this is a crucial part of a concierge's job. Days will be long, and concierges will interact with hundreds of people, and every interaction must be enthusiastic, energetic, and positive. It's required. They must be pleasers—and hospitality must be engrained in them. It's an attitude they either already have or they don't. We can train them to do the skills of the job, but we can't train their attitude.

My close colleague Amy pointed out something interesting. Without fail, she can predict if I like a candidate or not, based purely on the short walk from when I greet them at the reception desk to my office.

"How?" I asked her.

"Because in those fifteen seconds," she said, "if the candidate is enthusiastic and making small talk, you always end up liking them. But the ones that follow behind you in complete silence are the ones you never have a good feeling about."

Hmm, I guess that fifteen-second first impression goes a long way!

KEEP IT IN THE FAMILY

I believe in nepotism. In fact, the highest form of flattery is when a team member refers a friend or family member to join our organization. I encourage everyone to make this company our own little nirvana—a place where we'd all want our family and friends to come and work.

For example, at one point, two of our servers, Bo and his wife Carolyn, and two of their children worked at Bell Harbor International Conference Center. It made me think about the dynamic that happens in a family and how it translates to a working culture. When we work together, it makes a difference in how we treat each other. All of us want to see our friends and family members succeed, and we're willing to do what it takes to help make that happen. This infuses positive energy and fun into our company's culture and promotes teamwork to the highest degree. Right now, I'm aware of at least eighty-eight family units working at Columbia Hospitality, and I think that's a wonderful compliment.

PUSH WITH REMINDERS

I often find that I believe more in people's abilities than they do. In general, we all can do more than we believe we can. Companies that have been in business for some length of time face a never-ending stream of "we've never done that before," or "we don't have the resources for that." While both of those statements may be true, I always take the opportunity to try and inspire team members. It's amazing what people can do when someone else believes in them and is willing to encourage them to succeed.

It's probably true that we don't have the resources, but it's also true that we can stretch ourselves further and dream to do more. I feel a big piece of my job is to be a coach—to empower people to take a different approach and change their perspective, and to remind them how great we always feel when we successfully complete a challenge.

Our company, like most, was built with an entrepreneurial spirit. And as time goes by, it's a challenge to maintain that spirit. My colleague Shelley and I have worked together for a number of years. In fact, she was the first hire at Columbia Hospitality. Sometimes she gets frustrated when she comes up against a situation that she's never faced before. I've always encouraged her by reminding her of all the accomplishments she's achieved under similar circumstances. As one foot goes in front of the other, I can see her getting more and more excited. When the project is completed, she's exceeded expectations and done an excellent job. It happens every single time.

ASK THE RIGHT QUESTIONS

Interviewing job candidates is one of my favorite things to do. By the time they get to me, they've passed through all the other screens, so I get to meet the ones who are most likely to become team members. I find that when I'm hiring people we really want, I'm more nervous than they are. I know they can do the job, but I want to know who they are. I want to know they'll fit into our company culture and, since it's a two-way street, I'm hoping they're interviewing me to see if we're the right fit for them.

I ask about their funniest business experiences. If a person can laugh at himself or herself, it shows he or she has a positive attitude. If a candidate asks for my example, I tell him or her about when we first started organizing international events. I met a Thai dignitary, H. E. Bootnum. He was very friendly and outgoing, spoke perfect English, and was a delight to show around. Every morning, I'd greet him with a big, "Hello, H. E.," and throughout our day, I would make sure we were taking good care of him.

"H. E., do you need anything?"
"H. E., is there anything we can get for you?"

He was gracious and enthusiastic, and I felt very comfortable with H. E. until the third day. On the third day, his assistant pulled me aside and asked if I knew his name was not H. E.

"What!" I exclaimed in horror.

She explained that "H. E." stood for "His Excellency." Wow, that was embarrassing. I'm thankful I can laugh about it today and am always reminded by this story to refer to people more formally unless told otherwise.

I'll ask a candidate what he or she daydreams about when the candidate is driving on the freeway. This is not a trick question. Who doesn't daydream in traffic? I ask what the three things are that would make this a fantastic place to work. "I don't know" is the wackiest answer I've heard, and I don't mean that in a good way. The three things that make this a fantastic place to work for me are a great team environment where people work together without politics or games; a thriving atmosphere of enthusiasm; and an intellectual honesty where we challenge each other for better results.

I listen for kernels about their family, within those dreaded human-resources legal limits, of course. I love learning how they met their significant other. That's a good jumping-off point, because it usually leads to great family stories and the interests they have outside of work. This is a chance for me to get to know them on a personal level. It helps me understand what really makes them tick, and stories are a great way to remember each person.

SAY WHAT YOU THINK

Most CEOs say they like people who are direct. A lot of people say they like people who are direct, but their actions show they don't really mean it, because those aren't the people they hire. People who are direct challenge situations. They say what they think, they answer questions honestly, and they tend not to sugar coat the truth. The team members I am closest to and most appreciative of disagree, challenge, and with passion tell me why I may be wrong.

The best team member knocks the door down, and sometimes it's the one you're standing behind. It's not a good place to be standing, but it's great when he or she tells you what you don't want to hear and persuades you to think differently. Many people see this style of communication as negative, difficult, even confrontational. Sometimes it is—and some see that as threatening. That's why so many companies are filled with brown-nosers—people who tell their boss what they want to hear and support an ego-driven culture. That's the way a lot of company leaders like it, though they'll never admit it.

People who are worried about angering others won't take risks. To me, that's not acceptable. Not telling the truth or withholding information is dishonest, though we often don't think of it that way in a work setting. More importantly, as leaders, we often don't create a setting where people feel safe enough to share their ideas.

At Columbia Hospitality, we've built a culture based on confidence and trust. It's how we derive the best creative ideas and get the best results. Confidence results in getting stuff done. I want my team to make decisions and implement them. I'd much rather ask someone, "Why did you do this?" instead of, "Why didn't you…?"

CULTIVATE BUDS

This is a story about being extraordinary—about doing what's right, despite the human resources manual. We have a concierge named Bud who exemplifies the confidence and willingness to take risks for the good of our guests.

Bud was on duty as concierge the night of a holiday party for a major local company. One of the executives had had too much to drink—was drunk, really—and Bud asked him politely if he could call the man a taxi. The guy replied, "No way."

The exec had a new car and wasn't willing to leave it in the parking garage. It made more sense to him to get on the highway in it and risk his own life, and anyone else's unlucky enough to be sharing the road. Oh, the irony. Time passed, and Bud continued to stall the man while feeding him cups of black coffee. Just short of begging the man to go home in a cab, Bud decided to take a different approach. At this point, the party was over, and most guests had gone home. It was just Bud and the exec, and Bud's persistence finally paid off.

Bud proposed the man let him drive him home in the man's car, and Bud would take the taxi home. The man agreed. "By the way, sir, where do you live?" Bud asked. It turned out it was thirty miles south. During the thirty-plus-mile drive, the exec confided that his girlfriend had been to the party and had left in a huff, telling the man he'd drunk too much. He asked Bud if, rather than taking him straight home, he would mind having breakfast with him at Denny's. Bud agreed. Last I checked, Bud's job description did not include this gesture. "Above and beyond" was taking a new form.

The two men filled up on a meal of eggs, bacon, and hash browns, and Bud finally delivered the man and his car safely home. The next morning, the executive must have recognized the night could have ended entirely differently if it weren't for Bud. He sent Bud a very gracious note. Later that day, Bud received an additional note from the man with a $100 Nordstrom gift card.

As far as Bud was concerned, he did nothing outside of the scope of his job. And doing his job, in his mind, did not warrant gifts or special thanks. He donated the gift card for a Columbia Hospitality team raffle.

Meanwhile, our director of human resources at the time also caught wind of the buzz and didn't see Bud's action in quite the same light. The company handbook states that it is against policy to drive a guest's car. Bud broke a rule which was written with the intention of protecting team members. She wrote a formal reprimand. She wasn't wrong. He did break a company rule. But he also protected a guest. Bud showed excellent judgment, and was with us for many more great years. Bud was the first team member to retire from Columbia Hospitality and often comes back to visit and attend events.

Life isn't black and white. That's a lesson we should all remember. We want to empower our team to be confident and make good choices that are in the best interests of our guests, themselves, and our company.

BE SMART, BREAK RULES

Encouraging risk is the solution for preventing boredom, keeping great team members, and creating excellent service on a very individual level.

What inspires risk taking in someone? Is it DNA? Is it the environment? Maybe both; maybe neither. As a leader, the bigger question is how do you assess someone's willingness to break the rules for the good of the company? If an opportunity to provide above-and-beyond customer service shows up, how do you know if someone will A) recognize it and B) take it? Is it possible to judge this in the small window of an interview? I think it's impossible.

As a leader, you have to demonstrate it, encourage it, and reward it. The key is to empower people. Make sure they know you trust them and are confident in their judgment. Sam Walton, founder of Walmart, said in his biography that his success was based on rule breaking. He said, "My first rule of business is 'Break the rules.'"

I like risk takers, and I want them in my organization. I want to hire smart people who tell me I'm full of it if I'm full of it. I want to be challenged so we can create the best ideas. I want to work with team members who are confident, honest, thoughtful, and bold. Rule breakers.

An example is, some time ago a call came in to one of our conference centers regarding a two-month contract for meeting space. It would require more space than the conference center could accommodate. Knowing the revenue opportunity this challenge presented, instead of replying that it wouldn't be possible, the team jumped into action. As a group they determined that if we supplemented the conference center with some vacant office space across the street, we could make it happen for the client. The team put a plan together, presented it to the client and won the business. Great job …except we didn't manage the office space across the street!

Luckily the owner of the conference center also owned the building across the street, and, after some persuasion, she too saw the benefit of temporarily loaning us the space. Our team took a big risk, and in the end it literally paid off. This contract became the single highest revenue-generating contract in our company's history and one of the best opportunities to creatively break the rules to figure out a win-win.

We have a team member handbook, which I hope everyone reads. It's full of good information, and it outlines our rules. But if a situation arises and the solution makes sense and still aligns with our values, I encourage throwing the handbook out—but only if the answer is *yes* to *all* four of these questions:

1. Is the solution in line with our values? (No exceptions.)
2. Does it make your job better as a team member?
3. Is it good for our guests?
4. Is it good for our company?

START YOUNG

In eighth grade, my buddy and I wanted to go to McCall, Idaho, and rent our own cabin at Ponderosa Park. My parents weren't going to foot the bill, so I needed to get a job. But I was only fourteen and too young by legal standards to work. So no one would give me a job. I'd have to create my own.

I'd done it before. My earliest memory of dabbling in entrepreneurialism was when I was six. We lived in Boise, and my parents were very social. They'd have dinner parties, and when guests arrived, I'd greet them at the door and tell them if they took off their shoes, I'd shine them and guarantee they'd be ready to go by the time they were ready to leave.

My self-created job made me a lot of money for a six-year-old.

But now, as an eighth grader, this was serious. I needed to make bank. My parents had taken me traveling and, at most airports, I'd notice the Skycaps. Boise's airport didn't have Skycaps, and I thought it should. I pitched my idea to the airport manager and said my friend and I would do it for tips. The airport manager agreed and provided uniforms and a cart. When cars pulled up, we'd run to the car, unload the baggage, and wheel it into the airport.

We couldn't drive, so we made a deal with a shuttle service. We'd ride our bikes to the Hotel Boise and, for a discounted rate, hitch a ride to the airport in an airport shuttle. We did this for two summers. It was much more lucrative than playing kick the can or baseball. And I found I was way better at business. We made enough money, and we got to go on our trip.

KNOW YOUR STRENGTHS

I love sports! Actually, let me clarify. I love attending huge sporting events and watching the pomp and circumstance of the catering and event production.

I tried sports as a kid, but that didn't work out so well. During my Little League stint, I spent a lot more time on the bench than on the field. I wanted to play, and it was really frustrating, so I took matters into my own hands and got Doug, my older brother, hired as the coach. I figured that would be a sure-fire way to get field time.

One day, my brother told me he had great news. I was really excited. He told me he was giving me the best job of all. He was making me the permanent business manger and scorekeeper. Apparently my strategy failed.

PAY IT FORWARD

I've been lucky. I've landed in front of some amazing teachers during the twists and turns of life. They've believed in me and invested their expertise in helping me move forward as an entrepreneur. When I was a freshman or sophomore in high school, I met Bill Bridenbaugh, a Boise Cascade executive who was fundamental in helping me develop my interest in business. I was active in Junior Achievement, a national organization that helps kids learn business and finance. Every year, Junior Achievement hosted a national sales competition, and I entered and won.

Mr. Bridenbaugh was a sales dynamo and took me under his wing. He helped me knock down doors, build confidence, and understand the dynamics of people, and, with the nuances of time, I learned the valued skills of patience and anticipation. The competition happened all over the country, and he traveled with me to cities like Dallas and Atlanta. A couple of times, he arranged for us to take a private jet. I thought that was pretty cool, and I remembered thinking, *this is something I aspire to.*

Mr. Bridenbaugh's time and energy were priceless, and I didn't take them for granted. I've tried to reciprocate by "paying it forward"—investing my time and energy in people I believe in.

Over the years, several team members have told me that they've considered me a mentor to them. There is almost nothing as flattering as hearing that. What's even more amazing is that they've stuck with me either as team members or great friends. Leasa, Shelley, Barb, Jean, Leonora, Cheryl, Helio, Marijana, Michael, Carolyn, Amy, Nicolette, Lenny, Juanita, Barbara, Carlos, Doris, Blanca and Alan – each of them started with me more than ten years ago, when their biggest responsibility was showing up to work on time. Each rose through the ranks, taking on greater roles and responsibilities. Each has made a lasting impact on how the company looks today and will likely have a greater influence on how it will look in the future.

Others have moved on and their experience at Columbia Hospitality has helped them achieve bigger roles on bigger stages, but they remain an important part of the fabric of our company. While those still here and those that have moved on tell me what they've learned from me, I have learned far more from each of them; truly, a lifetime of invaluable lessons. The best part is when the teacher becomes the student.

BE SPIRITED

One of the core values of our company, and one I admire greatly in others, is enthusiasm. To have a strong sense of adventure and willingness to learn—and to approach life with a sense of enthusiasm—in my opinion creates a perfect storm for success.

My parents were always learning. At sixty years old, my mom learned Spanish. Way late in life, my dad decided to change religions and learned the Bible in a whole new way. Learning and doing and living with enthusiasm is what kept them young and lively—even when things were hard or didn't go the way they'd hoped.

When I was twelve, my dad would take me with him on his business trips. He sold food products, and I got to watch him in action. My dad had a great passion for meeting and embracing people. It was the way he learned from them, and this was his way of spending time with me and teaching me how to understand people.

My dad was enthusiastic about everything, which inspired people. His sales philosophy was "sell the sizzle, not the steak." When there was a lull in excitement, he would create it. He'd make stuff up. Once, we were walking through the county fair in Idaho, which was an annual family tradition. They'd hand out free stuff like yardsticks. It was a really crowded day and my dad held the yardstick to the sky like a pointer. "I can't believe it—it's amazing," he said, as he gazed along the line of the yardstick. And sure enough, eventually someone would say, "It's so beautiful"—and yet there was nothing there except for my dad's unrivaled enthusiasm.

By creating excitement, there's also the opportunity to make really bad mistakes. Once, my dad spent a lot of time trying to find a use for sagebrush. It was everywhere, and he decided it would make great barbecue chips. It turned out it was carcinogenic. But that's not to say one shouldn't try new things.

LET GO

One of the skills I admire most in great leaders is having the ability to know when it's time to let go of the reins and turn them over to fresh leadership. My dad knew exactly when that time was. He'd built a successful regional business in food products and real estate and grew it into an international entity. In his sixties, he turned it over to my two older brothers, Skip and Doug, who displayed another set of skills that I admire in great leaders. They both worked hard to make it even more successful, and, admirably, they did it free of ego. Every day, both of them checked their egos at the door. They worked together all day, every day. And when two people spend that much time together, inevitably an array of issues arises. When they did, my brothers worked together to negotiate and compromise their way through them, both feeling like each won in the end. That's what it's all about—creating win-wins so everyone feels like what he or she invested was appreciated and respected.

Knowing when to let go translates outside business and into other aspects of life. Our family grew up in my mother's family home, where generations had lived before us. Since both my parents were deceased, the logical question arose as to whether or not to sell the house. Its walls held a lot of history, a lot of memories. But Mom and Dad told us not to feel obligated to keep it.

As a family, my brothers Skip and Doug, my sister Jane, and I decided to sell our childhood home, knowing that what our parents always said was true. Memories are made in a home—a house doesn't make the memories. We all felt it was time for us to let go of the house, taking those wonderful memories with us, so a new family could enjoy the time there and make new memories in their home.

KNOW THE POINT

Good ideas and great results come from simply being observant. The devil really is in the details, and it doesn't take a trained eye to see that. What it does take is a fresh perspective and someone to ask, "What's the point?"

While we take it for granted that a rule or protocol is in place for a good reason, that's often not the case. If it seems like there's no point to a certain rule or protocol, there often isn't. It simply requires one person pointing that out. We can move mountains here, people!

I've found the untrained eye of a teenager is a pretty good voice of reason. For example, some time ago

I invited our son, James (nineteen at the time), and two of his friends to lunch at the World Trade Center Seattle dining room, a property we manage. I told them the only cost of lunch was they had to come up with three ideas to improve the dining room. When it comes to food, teenagers take these tasks seriously.

We were seated at a table facing the kitchen. James noticed that the servers going in and out of the kitchen passed by a curtain pulled to the side of the door.

"Why is that curtain there?" he asked.

"It's meant to block guests from seeing into the kitchen," I told him.

"But it's open all the time. I can see into the kitchen. What's the point?"

Ahh, the wisdom. Once we put it up, we found it got in the way of servers coming in and out, so it was more convenient to keep it open, defeating the point of why we put it up! We reminded the team of its purpose, and it was as simple as that. Now, the curtain is closed.

Another of the boys noticed that the paint on the walls of the restaurant was scratched and that the windows were dirty. "I've looked at your prices on the menu," he said. "And for what you charge, the paint should be repaired and the windows cleaned." But it didn't stop there.

Three years later, one of the boys, Gabe, was at a restaurant in a prominent hotel we were involved in. He texted me: *Had nice time at your hotel. Menu typo 3rd item. Two periods [..].*

They pointed out some obvious mistakes we should have caught but didn't. Their insight was fresh and practical and free of workplace politics. I try to involve our kids and their friends in my business, because it's a fun way to give them a full frontal of what I do and a great way for me to make it that much better.

ELIMINATE "THE WORD"

Everyone has a word—a word that makes him or her cringe whenever it is spoken out loud. My mom's word was "hate." She would not allow me or my siblings or any of our friends to use it in her presence. It was the off-limits word in our house.

My word is "fine." It's one of those vanilla words that doesn't tell me anything. When you ask someone how he or she is doing, and that person replies, "Fine," what does that tell me? It's a placeholder—a wall to keep others out. If someone responds, "Fine," to a question you've asked, I feel that person basically said they don't care about the outcome; he or she doesn't care enough to discuss it any further. *Dismissed!* Maybe I'm projecting, but I'm one person on a crusade to eliminate all uses of the word "fine," unless it's in reference to china.

NEVER EXPLAIN,
NEVER COMPLAIN

Both my parents instilled the importance of listening. When my dad was sick, people would come to his bedside and ask how he was doing. He would say, "I'm doing great, though the doctor says it's nothing trivial." More often than not, people would respond, "Glad to hear that." There is a great example of not really listening.

At my mom's memorial service, everyone shared the same sentiment: "When I talked to her, it seemed like all she cared about was me." Both my parents had the ability to make whomever they were talking to feel like the only person in the room. They had laser-sharp focus when it came to giving their attention to whatever was being discussed. I wish I could do more of that.

Mom instilled several virtues, which I refer to as Mom's Magnificent Lessons, in her children. The one that comes to mind right now is: Never explain, never complain. She always said, "No use complaining—just make the best of it." Boy, did she follow this advice, particularly when diagnosed with lung cancer. She kept going full speed. In June of 2010, she joined us in London for James's graduation, and in August she came to our place in Lake Chelan. She never, *ever* let up—never, *ever* complained. She passed away just two months later in October. She just kept living every day with a sense of adventure and enthusiasm. To see such an example is very inspiring.

LISTEN WITH BOTH EARS

This is especially true when it comes to the mouth. Mom always said two ears and one mouth make us exceedingly well designed to listen—and yet, too often, we don't hear a word others say.

Most of us are very good at running our mouths at full capacity but can't seem to let our ears do their part. Ears take a back seat—underutilized, benched from the game. Well, get your helmet on and get in the game, because a wise sage said to me, "If you're talking, you're not listening, and if you're not listening, you're not learning." The tool is there and the advantage is ours for the taking.

In work, as in life, people appreciate knowing you genuinely care about them. One of the easiest ways to show them is by taking the time to listen. One night I was in my office when Lesbia, a housekeeping team member, came in. I asked how her evening was, and she told me she was really excited. She was going home to Ecuador and was stopping in Miami to see her brother. She hadn't seen him in thirty years.

The excitement in her voice was contagious. After she left my office, I thought about her every day. I wondered, what would be the first thing she'd say when she saw him? What would he think when he saw her? What would they talk about? Where would he take her for dinner? I couldn't wait to hear the story of their reunion.

When she returned, we talked for an hour—she talked, she cried, I listened, we laughed. I learned that she was compassionate and loved the beach, loved to cook, and makes a fantastic empanada. I learned it was the best trip of her life.

At the end of the story, she apologized for taking up so much of my time. I was stunned. "No," I said emphatically. "I was grateful for the privilege of listening."

UNDIVIDE YOUR ATTENTION

One of the things I see people often do is lose focus on the person who's talking to them. They're distracted. We're all distracted. I'm guilty, too. Maybe that's why it bothers me so much.

We can't get to our phones fast enough to answer a text, read the latest e-mail, or check our friend's Facebook status. That sends a pretty clear and negative message to the person sitting in front of us. Basically, our actions tell that person he or she is not that important. So, why not give the gift—and it is a gift—of undivided attention?

I got busted. Our son James had a bunch of his friends come to dinner. I've known several of them for a very long time. I grilled the new ones with the same questions I always ask: How is your love life? What is your favorite class?

Admittedly, I was thinking about work and not listening as carefully as I could have been—*should* have been. The next time James joined us, he was with Tess, one of the girls from that dinner. I started asking her questions again: Where are you from? How many siblings do you have? She said, "You know, you asked me that the last time we had dinner." Busted! Embarrassed, I responded, "Well, I didn't know I cared until I found out you were dating my son. Now I have to start over."

That day, I was reminded harshly that if you're just going through the motions, you'll get caught, and rightfully so. Being half-engaged in a conversation isn't fair to anyone. It sends a selfish message and wastes people's time. It lacks sincerity, and for me must be fixed!

KEEP IT SIMPLE

When I'm considering decisions and weighing options, I always ask myself a couple of questions:

- Would Jeni and James understand this? (This was a really useful measure when they were younger).
- Would they be proud or embarrassed by it?

Kids are a great measure of truth. They have no filter, don't operate through a façade and give quick, honest opinions.

I want our guests to experience the pure excitement of a child. If "the kids" don't get it, the guests won't get it—and most of all, it'll be clear that *we* didn't get it.

PROVIDE VETO POWER

Our family had a really exciting door open for us when Deanna received a job offer in London. It came with an emotional mix of absolute exhilaration and fear—and a lot for each of us to think about as we made this decision. I was eager, ready to walk through the door and see what happened on the other side. I knew there'd be challenges, and we'd all have to make adjustments, but this was a chance of a lifetime. It wouldn't last forever, so I felt like we should seize it. My vote was YES!

Deanna convened the family. *Everyone* in the family had to give his or her honest opinion and vote, because once the decision was made, we all had to live with it. Deanna's terms were that everyone's vote counted equally, and the vote to go to London had to be unanimous. Jeni was seventeen and entering her senior year of high school. At thirteen, James was an eighth grader. They were both surprised, as was I, that their vote counted just the same as Deanna's or mine. And because of that, they knew they needed to be thoughtful and really consider the impact of their decision.

I had my preconceived judgments. I really thought Jeni would be against the idea and that James would be all for it. Boy, what do I know? Jeni voted with an ecstatic *yes!* She had traveled internationally and looked at this as one big adventure—the sooner the better, was her mind-set.

James refused to vote. He declared that since he'd never been to London, he felt he could not vote for something he didn't know enough about. He was right. Two days later, he and Deanna got on a plane headed to Heathrow. Upon their return, James voted yes—and off we went on our bicontinental family adventure.

I was in awe. Deanna handled this situation marvelously, which paved the road to making the entire experience a success. We all owned a piece of the decision. We all had to be accountable for choosing it, even if we didn't like the choice we'd made. I learned a lifetime of lessons that day.

BE PRESENT AND QUIET

When we dined as a family, it was a big deal. Everyone was busy and we all juggled crazy schedules, so when the stars aligned, which didn't happen that often, Deanna and I tried to make it a big deal. And we loved to invite Jeni's and James's friends. We loved it because it's amazing what we learned about when they talked amongst their friends. They talked as if we were not in the room and we certainly didn't do anything to remind them that we were.

COMPARTMENTALIZE

President Kennedy was a master at compartmentalizing. If you read any of the countless biographies, he's described as one who could carry on torrid social affairs, then walk into the Oval Office and plot military strategy.

The successful leaders I admire can compartmentalize, and Deanna has always been the stronger of the two of us in that area. It's one of the twenty million things I greatly admire about her. As an international board member and business consultant, she compartmentalizes well and is easily able to turn her work and home life on and off.

I see it as such an important skill and overall strength because it keeps you in the moment and allows you to really focus on the issue at hand. For me, it's a struggle, but I'm working on it. And I know it will help me sleep better; I just know it.

PERSONALIZE PERSPECTIVE

Keeping things in perspective is one of the hardest challenges I think we as humans face. It's easy to put the blinders on and fall into the routine of work. It's what we do, it's what we know, and, hopefully, it's what we love. Work is important... until it's not.

One day, I was having lunch with four college buddies. While I was waiting at the table, I was thinking about a project that hadn't worked out well, despite the many things that were going great. I wished I could compartmentalize more, but I often find myself hauling the weight of business into my personal affairs. My four friends arrived, and we fell into conversation, catching up on family and life. The weight of the project started to lift. Then, one of the guys divulged that his wife's cancer had come back and it was very serious.

Suddenly, my mind said, "What project?" It was a hard hitting jolt of perspective. And, somehow, it always comes just when we most need to be reminded of what really matters in life.

TREATING PRISONERS
KINDLY WINS GIRLS

My family has had the greatest impact on my life. I think most successful people could make that claim, but even so, at the risk of sounding mundane, my parents and grandparents deserve a lot of credit. As I've said, my dad was a successful entrepreneur. I watched him build successful businesses, and his foundation was built on treating everyone nicely, no matter his or her status. It didn't matter if it was his most important client or someone struggling on the street. He consistently treated everyone like royalty, as if each person was the most important person in the world.

He learned that principle from my grandfather, Leo Falk. The family lived down the street from the Idaho state prison. Anyone who wanted to date my mom (Leo's youngest daughter) had to meet with Leo first. He'd take the prospective date on a walk down the road to the jail. They'd enter the stone-cold facility, pass by the guards, and walk the rows of cells. Leo would greet each of the prisoners as they walked by. He'd judge the boy's character based on how he treated the prisoners. Few of the courters passed the test—but I guess my dad was the exception. Not only did he pass, he went on to instill in all of us the value of always treating people with dignity and respect.

In every aspect of my life, I try to emulate the tenet of treating others how you want to be treated. It's golden. My family also strongly influenced the idea of giving back to the community—which can mean resources, time, or expertise. It was driven into my head how important it is that everyone in the community does his or her part. That's what makes it a better place to live. By volunteering, people get to know each other; new friends are made; new business results. It just makes good social and economic sense. Some of my closest friends are people I've met through community service and serving on boards. Our paths may never have crossed otherwise, and the value is enormous.

CHANGE IT UP

In 2002, when James was a fourth grader and Jeni was in eighth grade, Deanna and I decided to take a sabbatical. We decided she'd take the year off and I'd commute from Lake Chelan to the office in Seattle. While Lake Chelan is only a couple of hours from Seattle, I can tell you, we were a long way from Mercer Island, WA.

We enrolled our children in a school where they learned about agriculture and what it was like to live in a small town. When James came home, he'd go sailing or fishing. When he'd catch fish, he'd deliver them to the neighbors for their dinner. (In truth, no one in our family liked cleaning fish).

119

What surprised me was how amazing life was without all the daily stimulation that gets enmeshed in our surroundings. Our family loves going out to dinner or to concerts in the city. But we had just as much fun playing board games together. Or we'd invite our neighbors over to play with us, which has resulted in lifelong friendships.

What also surprised me was how simple it was to conduct business from afar. I think delegating is a compliment to the team. It shows how much you trust their decisions. And when I was out of the office, everyone had the opportunity to be the big cheese. It worked. And the experience, or experiment, really, was the fabric that allowed our family to experience the opportunity in London.

SLEEP BETTER

What keeps me up at night? All the wrong things. Sometimes it's hard to maintain the perspective that you've done the best you can—and that it's only business. I spend too much time lying in bed at 2 a.m. thinking about that day's meeting or worrying about the next day. I think about how, as the company continues to grow, we are going to maintain our quality standards and deliver on our values at every property. I should be thinking about how to improve my golf game, or the other fantasies I know some of my buddies think about at 2 a.m.

I think about people a lot. I wonder if every single person who has been in contact with us is having an amazing experience. I worry whether we've been completely fair to every single person. It's getting harder to keep track of everything as we grow and add people and properties. In the end, others are doing the hiring, but I can sleep better knowing they're excellent leaders whom I trust. I can't know everything.

OPEN DOORS

Opening doors for others is something I take literally. And I love it when others do, too. If I could do any job in hospitality for a day, I would love to be a concierge in a five-star hotel. That's where I'd have the power to be magical and exceed guests' expectations. You can show that the thing most people think can't be done...*can*.

I travel a lot and have been absolutely blown away by some of the concierges I've encountered. The first time this happened, I was in New York at the Hotel Plaza Athenee. I was headed to a black-tie event and, just before it was time to leave, I realized I'd forgotten to pack my bow tie.

I called down to the concierge to find out where I might be able to buy one—*quickly*. The person I spoke with made it sound like he got that request all the time, which helped make me feel a little less stupid and gave me the confidence that he knew how to fix it. As directed, I came downstairs and found about ten waiters lined up military style, all wearing a selection of bow ties. "Take your pick," said the concierge. It was perfect.

KNOW YOUR RULES

My Fifteen Personal Rules of Doing Business are:

1. Follow values every day—they are the litmus test for every decision you make.
2. Tune in and go with your gut—if it doesn't feel right, it probably isn't.
3. Know which vowels are more important. A good leader limits the *I*s and concentrates on the *U*s. Cliché or not, it's true—there is no *I* in *team*.
4. We've got one mouth and two ears for a reason. Listen harder.

5. Don't take it too seriously—know your priorities and keep perspective.

6. Take risks—make mistakes, learn, and keep moving forward.

7. Don't chew your cabbage twice, meaning don't keep rehashing. Move on.

8. Don't be stale—shake it up regularly and make changes.

9. Once you're in the company family, you're in the family. Not exactly Mafioso, but loyalty is a two-way street.

10. Be who you are, and give people the honor of getting to know you.

11. Be smart and decisive.

12. Write thank-you notes immediately.

13. Ask more questions and give fewer answers.

14. Pick up the phone more often than you e-mail.

15. Have a blast every day!

EPILOGUE

Thank you

If you've made it this far, I feel like thanking you is the least I can do. I truly appreciate that you devoted time to reading these thoughts. I am grateful for the opportunity to create experiences, open doors, and grow with so many wonderful people.

Through the original process of writing this book and with this update, I continue to realize how incredibly lucky I am. I've learned a lot about life and people and the things that make for a good story but are not fit to print. Most importantly, I have a stronger understanding and deeper appreciation for my family — Deanna, Jeni, and James—as well as my second family—all my colleagues and friends at Columbia Hospitality and elsewhere.

We've truly come a long way! And I thank every-one who spent time on the journey with me. Doors open, doors close, but relationships remain con-stant, and for that, I am forever grateful.

ABOUT THE AUTHOR

John Oppenheimer is a travel and tourism visionary and entrepreneur with a passion for the hospitality industry. He has founded five successful hospitality-related businesses.

John currently serves on the Board of the Virginia Mason Medical Center Foundation, where he is the Chair, as well as the Western Region Advisory Board of Northern Trust, and the 5th Avenue Theatre Board of Directors. He is a past Chapter Chair of the World President's Organization (WPO) and past chairman of the Woodland Park Zoo Board of Directors. He is also a past member of the Greater Seattle Chamber of Commerce Board of Trustees, the Junior Achievement Board of Directors, the Fred Hutchinson Cancer Research Center Foundation Board, and the Washington Council on International Trade.

John and his wife of 32 years, Deanna, are past honorees of Seattle Hotel Association's Evening of Hope Gala and have served as co-chairs of many civic events including the Woodland Park Zoo Jungle Party, the Virginia Mason Dreambuilders' Ball, and the Junior Achievement Puget Sound Business Hall of Fame event.

John graduated from the University of Puget Sound with degrees in Urban Affairs and Political Science. He and Deanna were recently honored for their continued service and philanthropy to their alma mater with the dedication of Oppenheimer Hall. They reside in Seattle, Washington and have two adult children, Jeni and James.

35342836R00080

Made in the USA
Middletown, DE
05 February 2019